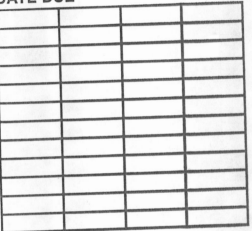

DATE DUE

What Scares Me

& What I Do About It

Stories & Pictures by Sunday School Kids

Edited by Jeff Kunkel

WHAT SCARES ME AND WHAT I DO ABOUT IT
Stories and Pictures by Sunday School Kids

Large-quantity purchases or custom editions of this book are available at a discount from the publisher. For more information, contact the sales department at Augsburg Fortress, Publishers, 1-800-328-4648, or write to: Sales Director, Augsburg Fortress, Publishers, P.O. Box 1209, Minneapolis, MN 55440-1209.

ISBN 0-8066-4558-X

Cover design by Laurie Duren Design; Book design by Michelle L. N. Cook

The paper used in this publication meets the minimum requirements of American National Standard for Information Sciences—Permanence of Paper for Printed Library Materials, ANSI Z329.48-1984. ⊛ ™

Manufactured in Singapore.

07   06   05   04   03   1   2   3   4   5   6   7   8   9   10

"Tornadoes, like the one
in my picture, scare me."
—picture by Aisha Ivery, age 12

Contents

Introduction

Many kids, like adults, are reluctant to name or explore their fears. On the other hand, many kids, like adults, will happily name and explore their fears if they are invited to do so, feel safe to do so, and sense that they have something to gain by doing so. This is what I did with kids featured in this book. First, I invited them to name their fears, and I wrote down each fear in big, colorful letters for all to see—dozens and dozens of fears! Next, I asked each child to choose one of the fears on the list to talk about and draw or paint. For this book, I chose twenty-one of these fears and divided them this way: At Home, At School, Out and About, and Other Worlds.

picture by Nathaniel Griffen, age 8

Next, I invited each child to talk about and draw or paint what he or she does to diminish or better face that fear. Almost without exception, the kids came up with ingenious and practical ways of facing that fear. Some of these ways had to do with things they could do: turn on the lights, call for Mom, call 911, say a prayer, read a Bible story, etc. Some of these ways had to do with shaping how they thought about a fear or repeating a slogan or motto to themselves.

The kids in my StoryArt groups discovered that there are real benefits to naming and facing their fears. First, they discovered that they aren't the only ones in the world with fears inside them—that other kids have fears, too! This was demonstrated again and again by the energy and laughter that accompanied the listing of the fears! One nine-year-old boy cried out in glee,

"I never knew anyone else was afraid of water!" Second, kids discovered that naming and exploring the fear brings clarity to the fear and drains it of some power. One eight-year-old girl said it this way, "When I talk about or draw my fear, the fear gets smaller, and I get bigger." Most kids also discovered that there are lots of ways to face a fear and do something about it.

picture by Jacob Jones, age 10

The nearly sixty kids who have comments or artwork featured in this book have attended one of my StoryArt workshops. These kids come from many different races and backgrounds and five states: Missouri, Alaska, California, Oregon, and Illinois. These kids range in age from three to fifteen and come from different parts of the Christian tradition: Lutheran, United Methodist, Presbyterian, Roman Catholic, and Russian Orthodox.

Let the kids in this book inspire you—and the children in your life—to thought, prayer, and action in the face of fear!

Jeff Kunkel

Jeff Kunkel

The Dark Scares Me

"I get scared of the dark, especially if I'm alone. Dark shadows on the wall scare me, too, because they move and look like ghosts."

—Alexandria Friske, age 9

picture by Alexandria Friske, age 9

picture by Paige Cummins, age 6

"This is a picture of me in my bed. The dark scares me because I can't see anything, but I can hear lots of noises—things that go thump, and I don't know what is making the thump."

—Paige Cummins, age 6

What I Do about It

picture by Rachel Hoiem, age 7

"I say this Bible verse to myself, 'God has not given me a spirit of fear but of power, love, and a sound mind.'"
—Ben Sutton, age 10

"I got to thinking about monsters and ghosts and called my parents into my bedroom. They turned on the lights and made me feel better."
—Rachel Hoiem, age 7

"I keep a flashlight by my bed, and if I see a dark shadow in my room, I shine my light on it, which makes it disappear and lets me know that it's only a shadow and not a ghost."
—Alexandria Friske, age 9

picture by Alexandria Friske, age 9

Nightmares Scare Me

"I was on the Screaming Eagle once, and the roller coaster was broken and kept going around and around—it wouldn't stop! I yelled, 'Help!' This is a picture of me having a nightmare about that roller coaster ride."
—Ashley Cummins, age 8

picture by Ashley Cummins, age 8

picture by Audrey Huetteman, age 9

"This is me having a nightmare about a pink robot, which is trying to shoot me with his gun."
—Audrey Huetteman, age 9

What I Do about It

picture by Audrey Huetteman, age 9

"If a nightmare wakes me up, I try to think about something happy. In this picture, I'm thinking about going to a birthday party and swimming, and this helps me go back to sleep."
—Ashley Cummins, age 8

"When I wake up from a nightmare, I turn on my night-light so that I can look around and see that everything is okay."
—Audrey Huetteman, age 9

"I remember the Bible story about Daniel. God kept Daniel safe all night—and Daniel was in a den of lions!"
—Kelly Reed, age 11

picture by Ashley Cummins, age 8

Bad Storms Scare Me

"This is a picture of our house. It's daytime, but there's such a bad storm that it is as dark as midnight, and two tornadoes are heading toward the house. Tornadoes can suck your house into the sky!"
—Christian Williams, age 8

picture by Christian Williams, age 8

picture by Hannah Conley, age 6

"This is me and my family by our backyard pond. The sky is black and full of clouds and lightning. Some horses near here got killed by lightning, and it can kill people, too."
—Hannah Conley, age 6

What I Do about It

picture by Jaime Wright, age 7

"This is an angel in heaven watching a storm on earth. When I get scared by a storm, I like to remember that the angels are still watching over me."
—Jaime Wright, age 7

"This is me and my family in the basement, where we go to keep safe in a bad storm, even though lightning can still come through the basement window and start a fire."
—Hannah Conley, age 6

picture by Hannah Conley, age 6

Being Alone Scares Me

"This is me in my bedroom. I don't like to be all alone in a room."
—Emily Johnson, age 7

"My house is so full of people that I'm not used to being alone."
—Joel Armando Saavedra, age 7

picture by Emily Johnson, age 7

What I Do about It

picture by Ashley Cummins, age 8

"If I'm alone and safe, I can play or read or sing all by myself."
—Ashley Cummins, age 8

"I can say my favorite prayer, 'Dear God, please bless . . .' and then I say the name of each person I want God to bless."
—Kilan Bishop, age 10

"I pray all alone in my room."
—Colin Davis, age 10

picture by Colin Davis, age 10

Dad Yelling, Mom Crying Scares Me

"Once, I was watching a movie with Mom, and she started crying, which scared me. Mom's dad died when she was little, and this movie was about a young girl whose dad died."
—Sophia Hanson-Richter, age 7

picture by Sophia Hanson-Richter, age 7

picture by Tony Falkowski, age 9

"This is Dad blowing his top! I get scared when he yells, because I know something bad has happened."
—Tony Falkowski, age 9

What I Do about It

picture by Maddie Crawford, age 7

"This is our family all together, happy."
—Alysandre Saavedra, age 10

"If Mom cries, I want to know why she's crying, so I ask her a lot of questions and we talk and both feel better."
—Audrey Huetteman, age 9

"When Dad yells, I try to help him, but if I can't, I go to my room and say a prayer that everything will be okay."
—Tony Falkowski, age 9

picture by Alysandre Saavedra, age 10

Intruders Scare Me

"Sometimes, I get scared of someone breaking into our house. In my picture, there's a robber with a black mask in my room. I'm hiding from him in the closet."
—Liz James, age 9

"On the television, I heard about a kidnapper coming right into a girl's room and taking her."
—Emily Johnson, age 7

picture by Liz James, age 9

picture by Frank Ahio, age 15

"This is a picture of a masked guy who just robbed someone's house. He's running away with a bag of money in one hand and a gun in the other. There's graffiti painted on the wall behind him."
—Frank Ahio, age 15

What I Do about It

picture by Emily Johnson, age 7

"This is a picture of me and my parents. We're talking about how to keep our house safe and keep out kidnappers."
—Emily Johnson, age 7

"I help to keep our house and yard looking good and keep an eye on strangers."
—Frank Ahio, age 15

picture by Liz James, age 9

"This picture shows the same robber coming toward our house, but now we have a dog—and the barking will scare him away."
—Liz James, 9

Fire Scares Me

"I'm scared of any big fire, like the house on fire in my picture."
—Malia Lupe Nai, age 6

picture by Malia Lupe Nai, age 6

picture by Carter Price, age 3

"Fire moves around and can hurt you."
—Carter Price, age 3

What I Do about It

picture by Katie Reutter, age 11

"If I see a fire, I can call 911 and tell them about the fire. That's what the people in my picture did—and now the firefighters are there and putting out the fire. One firefighter is rescuing a cat from an upstairs window."
—Katie Reutter, age 11

picture by Megan Stover, age 14

"If a fire is small, I can put it out with a fire extinguisher before anyone gets hurt."
—Megan Stover, age 14

"This is how I'll look if I let my mom do my hair! How embarrassing!"
—Malia Bishop, age 9

picture by Malia Bishop, age 9

picture by Alex Morelan, age 10

"I'm scared of starting a new grade and not knowing who my teacher will be."
—Alex Morelan, age 10

picture by Malia Bishop, age 9

"If I do my hair myself, I'll look good and be happy."
—Malia Bishop, age 9

picture by Alysandre Saavedra, age 10

"On my first day of school, I take a little gift to my teacher and try to make at least one new friend."
—Alysandre Saavedra, age 10

Bullies Scare Me

"Bullies scare me because they are much bigger than me, and they can hurt me or take my lunch money."
—Alysha Rhodes, age 9

picture by Alexandria Friske, age 9

"I get scared by boys ganging up on me."
—Alexandria Friske, age 9

picture by Alysha Rhodes, age 9

What I Do about It

picture by Xi ahn Mankin, age 4

"In this picture, the bully is red and mean. I go and get Dad and hold his hand, and we walk away."
—Xi ahn Mankin, age 4

picture by Dorian Peters, age 10

"If bullies come after me, I can ignore them, run away, invite my friends to be with me—like in my picture—or tell a teacher."
—Dorian Peters, age 10

Teachers Scare Me

"This is a picture of my music class with my teacher, drum, blackboard, xylophones, and a very rare xylophone at the far right. I'm scared of my teacher because she shouts a lot into a microphone, and she's not patient. Sometimes she makes me sing in front of the whole class."
—Audrey Huetteman, age 9

picture by Audrey Huetteman, age 9

picture by Nathaniel Griffen, age 8

"I'm afraid of my teacher because she gives so much homework that I don't always get it done."
—Nathaniel Griffen, age 8

What I Do about It

picture by Audrey Huetteman, age 9

"This is a picture of me and my friend, Ellie, on my way to class. I tell her that I don't like to be shouted at by my teacher and Ellie understands. Other things I do to be less afraid:
1. Take deep breaths.
2. Say to myself, 'It's okay.'"
—Audrey Huetteman, age 9

picture by Vanessa Morelan, age 8

"My teacher asks me to do so many special favors for her that I don't get my own work done. Sometimes, I tell her, 'Please ask someone else.'"
—Vanessa Morelan, age 8

Hard Subjects Scare Me

"This is me in my desk, holding a book. I'm scared of reading out loud, because I won't know how to say certain words and the other kids will have to help me."
—Zachary Campbell, age 8

picture by Zachary Campbell, age 8

picture by Jessie Horvath, age 15

"This is a picture of with a lot of letters swirling around. Spelling is easy for lots of kids, but it's hard for me. I'm afraid to write on the blackboard because everyone will see the words I can't spell right."
—Jessie Horvath, age 15

What I Do about It

picture by Emily Johnson, age 7

"I'm less scared of reading now that I'm seeing a reading tutor. That's me on the left and her on the right with a table between us. We're practicing."
—Emily Johnson, age 7

"I get scared of math class because it's hard, and I don't always know the right answer. If I study a lot, I do better."
—Scott Campbell, age 10

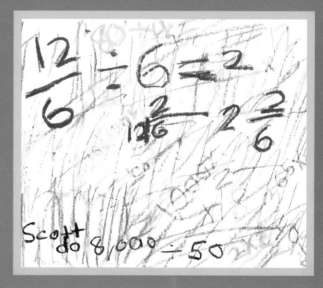

picture by Scott Campbell, age 10

Tests & Contests Scare Me

"Tests make me nervous. What if I don't know the answers to the problems? What if I don't pass? What if I fail or get a bad grade?"
—Zachary Campbell, age 8

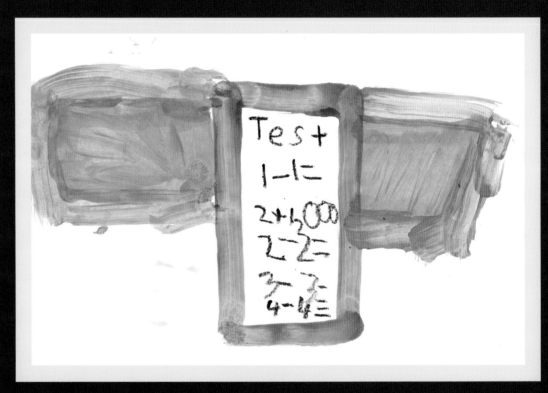

picture by Zachary Campbell, age 8

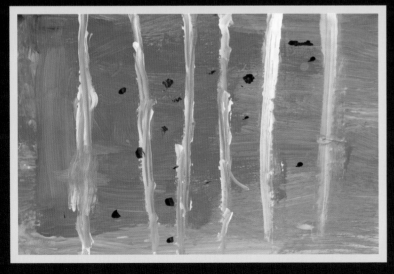

picture by Everett Williams, age 11

"My painting shows a football game from high up, with green grass, yard lines, and brown players. One of the players just had a pass thrown to him—but he dropped the ball."
—Everett Williams, age 11

What I Do about It

picture by Kelsey Thompson, age 9

"There's a Bible story about a life and death contest between a giant warrior named Goliath and a shepherd boy named David. Goliath has steel armor, a shield, and a mighty spear. David has a little slingshot. Surprise! David wins—he cracks Goliath's skull with a stone from his slingshot. I like this story because David, the little guy, wins."
—Kelsey Thompson, age 9

picture by Sarah Williams, age 6

"One way to be less afraid of tests is to take a practice test before the real one. In this picture, a teacher has put a practice test on the chalkboard."
—Sarah Williams, age 6

"If I expect to catch the ball, I have to practice catching it. The pros practice all the time, and sometimes they still drop the ball!"
—Everett Williams, age 11

Sharp Teeth Scare Me

"Snakes scare me because they have fangs and poison like the one I drew."
—Emily Pickens-Jones, age 15

picture by Emily Pickens-Jones, age 15

picture by Jenna Nibert, age 8

"This is me being scared of a dog, even though my jaw doesn't drop that far."
—Jenna Nibert, age 8

What I Do about It

picture by Liz James, age 9

"I live in the mountains, and we have lots of rattlesnakes. I'm less afraid of them now that I've learned more about how to act if I see one. First, I stay still if I see one—they can't see well. Second, I stay at least six feet away—that's their striking range."
—Liz James, age 9

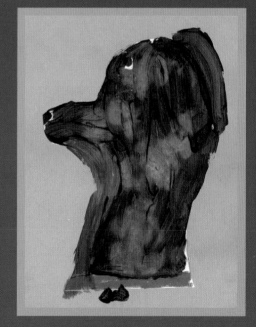

picture by Hannah Leigh Burnett, age 9

"When I want to play with a dog, I find Sarah. She likes me and would protect me if another dog tried to hurt me."
—Hannah Leigh Burnett, age 9

"If a dog comes up to me, I just stand still and act like a tree. They sniff me and go away."
—Dorian Peters, age 10

Heights & Depths Scare Me

"Even though I'm afraid of heights, I love to climb trees. Sometimes, like in this picture, I climb too high, get scared, and can't get down. I'm stuck!"
—Morgan Stover, age 11

"I'm afraid of the ocean, because once I was playing along the beach and a big wave came up behind me and knocked me underwater, and I couldn't breathe or see."
—Joel Armando Saavedra, age 7

picture by Joel Armando Saavedra, age 7

picture by Morgan Stover, age 11

What I Do about It

picture by Morgan Stover, age 11

"I can learn to climb to a lower branch, so I don't get scared and stuck."
—Morgan Stover, age 11

picture by Katie Reutter, age 11

"One time, two boys were in a pool without a lifeguard, trying to see who could stay underwater the longest. Both boys passed out and almost drowned. When I swim, I make sure there is a lifeguard, and I never play dangerous games in the water."
—Katie Reutter, age 11

Getting Lost Scares Me

"If I went into the woods by myself, I'd get lost and scared."
—Katie Reutter, age 11

picture by Katie Reutter, age 11

picture by Jani Mudd, age 10

"That's me in a store. Once, I got lost there, by the bottles of fingernail polish."
—Jani Mudd, age 10

What I Do about It

picture by Katie Reutter, age 11

"If I want to go for a hike, I go with someone like my mom to make sure I don't get lost."
—Katie Reutter, age 11

picture by Jani Mudd, age 10

"Now, I stay closer to Mom in the store and don't wander off."
—Jani Mudd, age 10

Bad Accidents Scare Me

"I'm afraid of breaking a bone while skate-boarding. This guy is dropping in a half pipe, does a back flip, and breaks his leg."
—Ben Sutton, age 10

"I've seen two car crashes and people got hurt bad, so I worry about us getting into a crash."
—Nathaniel Griffen, age 8

picture by Ben Sutton, age 10

picture by Kilan Bishop, age 10

"I'm afraid of going down big hills on my bike, because once I got going too fast, hit a log, and flew off my bike, head first."
—Kilan Bishop, age 10

What I Do about It

picture by Jenna Nibert, age 8

"To avoid accidents, the driver of the car should pay attention to the road and not use a cell phone or a laptop."
—Jenna Nibert, age 8

"I can put on kneepads to avoid getting hurt while skateboarding."
—Jacob Jones, age 10

picture by Kilan Bishop, age 10

"I don't go down steep hills on my bike now."
—Kilan Bishop, age 10

Weapons Scare Me

"Today, there was a shooting near my Grandma's house. A man shot a woman at the grocery store, then shot himself. Guns kill, that's why they scare me."
—Malia Bishop, age 9

"I don't like people getting stabbed, because I don't like people hurt or dead."
—Kayla Huetteman, age 7

picture by Malia Bishop, age 9

picture by Matthew Izzo, age 10

"This is a picture of a person pointing a gun at his friend. He thought the gun was unloaded, so he pulled the trigger—and guess what? The gun was loaded and he shot his friend."
—Matthew Izzo, age 10

What I Do about It

picture by Tasi Ahio, age 12

"I painted a handgun, a knife, and a grenade with a red "X" across each one to show that weapons are not allowed around me. If I see someone with a weapon, I will run away and tell my dad or a teacher."
—Tasi Ahio, age 12

"I don't threaten anyone, because they might threaten me back, and they might have some kind of weapon. Maybe I should go to a gun store and protest, because guns are too easy to buy. If I ever heard a gunshot, I'd run away and call 911."
—Malia Bishop, age 9

Terrorists Scare Me

"Terrorists are people who hate us and want to kill us. This drawing shows the Twin Towers in New York being attacked by terrorists with airplanes. The buildings are on fire. People are jumping out of windows with parachutes, and a fireman is trying to put out the fire."
—Nicky Reed, age 8

"I cried when I heard about the attacks, because everyone in the airplanes and lots of people in the buildings got killed. It's sad and scary, because this might happen again and other people will get killed."
—Kayla Huetteman, age 7

picture by Nicky Reed, age 8

What I Do about It

picture by Ivan Arriaga, age 10

"This is a police car on it's way to stop something really bad from happening. I know that I can call 911 anytime and the police will come."
—Ivan Arriaga, age 10

"I say this prayer: Dear God, please keep me safe from anything that may harm me. Protect every innocent person and bless those in trouble."
—Kilan Bishop, age 10

picture by Frank Ahio, age 15

"I try to remember that no matter what happens, God has us all in his hands, like this."
—Frank Ahio, age 15

"If I could, I'd hit the pause button so that a terrorist attack wouldn't happen."
—Ben Reutter, age 8

Death Scares Me

"This is a skull and crossbones, a sign of death. I drew it this way, because people are afraid of anything that's large, spiky, or poisonous."
—Daniel Parks, age 9

"Death is scary. My great-grandpa died, and I went to see him at the funeral home. He was real quiet and didn't move at all."
—Ivan Arriaga, age 10

picture by Daniel Parks, age 9

picture by Daniel Parks, age 9

"Wherever the Grim Reaper goes, death follows. He's dressed in black, carries a scythe, and draws his sense of power from a blue and red sign above the earth."
—Daniel Parks, age 9

What I Do about It

picture by Ethan Mahoney, age 5

"This is me and God. I'm sticking my hand into God so that I can use his power and love."
—Ethan Mahoney, age 5

"Mom and Dad asked me, 'Do you want to go to your friend's grave and put flowers on it?' I said, 'No, if I go there I might die, too.' They said, 'No, you won't get his disease and die. You are young and healthy and will live a long time.' So we went and put flowers on my friend's grave."
—Audrey Huetteman, age 9

"In Psalm 23, the Lord is called, 'My Shepherd.' This is a picture of a shepherd leading his sheep, just like God leads us. The Psalm says that God will even lead us through the Valley of Death."
—Emma Lambert, age 8

picture by Emma Lambert, age 8

The Devil Scares Me

"The devil is mean and full of lies. He doesn't want you to love God, he wants you to love the devil. He can talk to you inside your mind and make you think that you are hearing God talk to you."
—Jacob Jones, age 10

picture by Jacob Jones, age 10

picture by Rene Jaquith, age 9

"The devil used to be an angel in heaven, but God kicked him out because the devil didn't know how to love. The devil wants to get back into heaven, but he wants to find a shortcut—and he wants us to take the shortcut with him."
—Ben Sutton, age 10

"The devil is red, pink, green, and black. He uses his pitchfork to make people do what he wants them to do."
—Rene Jaquith, age 9

What I Do about It

picture by Sarah Gist, age 9

"In this picture, God is the white light, and the devil is the snake, and they are talking about God's servant, a guy named Job. The devil made a lot of trouble for Job, but God didn't let the devil hurt Job, and God doesn't let the devil hurt me."
—Sarah Gist, age 9

picture by Kelly Reed, age 11

"The devil is afraid of God, so when I'm afraid of the devil, I go to church. That's my church, full of people. I'm inside the church, and the devil is outside, afraid to go in."
—Kelly Reed, age 11

Monsters & Aliens & Ghosts Scare Me

"I don't know if aliens really exist, but that doesn't stop me from being spooked by the thought of them. My chalk pastel drawing shows an alien in a flying saucer, looking for a landing place on earth. I hope it's not in my backyard!"
—Reed Mankins, age 12

picture by Reed Mankins, age 12

picture by Audrey Twilleager, age 5

"This a monster chasing me."
—Audrey Twilleager, age 5

What I Do about It

picture by Audrey Twilleager, age 5

"This is a picture of a monster. I would stick out my tongue at him to show him I'm not that scared."
—Audrey Twilleager, age 5

"I like to draw pictures of what scares me because then I'm not so scared."
—Rose Iwahashi, age 6

"I have to stay away from scary movies. If I do go to one, I have to close my eyes and plug my ears a lot."
—Audrey Huetteman, age 9

Writers & Artists

Christine Ledford, age 12, Oakland, California, cover
Aisha Ivery, age 12, El Cerrito, California, cover, 2
Jaime Wright, age 7, Sacramento, California, 1, 11
Sophia Hanson-Richter, age 7, McMinnville, Oregon, 1, 14
Jenna Nibert, age 8, Pleasanton, California, 3, 30, 37
Nathaniel Griffen, age 8, Hannibal, Missouri, 4, 24, 36
Jacob Jones, age 10, Hannibal, Missouri, 5, 37, 44
Alexandria Friske, age 9, McHenry, Illinois, 6, 7, 22
Paige Cummins, age 6, Hannibal, Missouri, 6
Rachel Hoiem, age 7, Oakland, California, 7
Ben Sutton, age 10, Hannibal, Missouri, 7, 36, 44
Ashley Cummins, age 8, Hannibal, Missouri, 8, 9, 13
Audrey Huetteman, age 9, San Leandro, California, 8, 9, 15, 24, 25, 43, 47
Kelly Reed, age 11, Alameda, California, 9, 45
Hannah Conley, age 6, Hannibal, Missouri, 10, 11
Christian Williams, age 8, Hannibal, Missouri, 10
Emily Johnson, age 7, Oakland, California, 12, 16, 17, 27
Joel Armando Saavedra, age 7, San Jose, California, 12, 32
Kilan Bishop, age 10, Sacramento, California, 13, 36, 37, 41
Colin Davis, age 10, Berkeley, California, 13
Tony Falkowski, age 9, South San Francisco, California, 14, 15
Maddie Crawford, age 7, Concord, California, 15
Alysandre Saavedra, age 10, San Jose, California, 15, 21
Liz James, age 9, La Grange, California, 16, 17, 31
Frank Ahio, age 15, Millbrae, California, 16, 17, 41
Malia Lupe Nai, age 6, Sacramento, California, 18
Carter Price, age 3, Unalaska, Alaska, 18
Megan Stover, age 14, Hannibal, Missouri, 19
Katie Reutter, age 11, Walnut Creek, California, 19, 33, 34, 35
Malia Bishop, age 9, Sacramento, California, 20, 21, 38, 39

Alex Morelan, age 10, Campbell, California, 20
Alysha Rhodes, age 9, Hannibal, Missouri, 22
Xi ahn Mankin, age 4, Oakland, California, 23
Dorian Peters, age 10, Hannibal, Missouri, 23, 31
Vanessa Morelan, age 8, Campbell, California, 25
Jessie Horvath, age 15, Campbell, California, 26
Zachary Campbell, age 8, San Jose, California, 26, 28
Scott Campbell, age 10, Campbell, California, 27
Everett Williams, age 9, Loomis, California, 28, 29
Sarah Williams, age 6, Walnut Creek, California, 29
Kelsey Thompson, age 9, Los Altos, California, 29
Emily Pickens-Jones, age 15, Burlingame, California, 30
Hannah Leigh Burnett, age 9, Dublin, California, 31
Morgan Stover, age 11, Hannibal, Missouri, 32, 33
Jani Mudd, age 10, Hannibal, Missouri, 34, 35
Matthew Izzo, age 10, Sacramento, California, 38
Kayla Huetteman, age 7, San Leandro, California, 38, 40
Tasi Ahio, age 12, Milbrae, California, 39
Nicky Reed, age 8, Alameda, California, 40
Ivan Arriaga, age 10, San Leandro, California, 41, 42
Ben Reutter, age 8, Walnut Creek, California, 41
Daniel Parks, age 9, Santa Clara, California, 42
Ethan Mahoney, age 5, Unalaska, Alaska, 43
Emma Lambert, age 8, Crystal Lake, Illinois, 43
Rene Jaquith, age 9, Berkeley, California, 44
Sarah Gist, age 9, Los Altos, California, 45
Rose Iwahashi, age 6, Sacramento, California, 47
Reed Mankins, age 12, Sacramento, California, 46
Audrey Twilleager, age 5, Campbell, California, 46, 47